HOW TO WRITE COMPANY NEWSLETTERS

by

Gerene Reid

Published by TIB PUBLICATIONS

2922 North State Road 7, Margate, Florida 33063

Second Edition
First Printing 1977

Copyright © 1980 by Gerene Reid

All rights reserved. This book may not be reproduced or utilized in any form by any means without written permission from the publisher.

Library of Congress Number: 79-66676
ISBN: 0-931882-08-7

Printed in the United States of America

Published by TIB PUBLICATIONS
2922 North State Road 7, Margate, Florida 33063

HOW TO WRITE COMPANY NEWSLETTERS
TABLE OF CONTENTS

Preface 4

Introduction.................................... 5

House Organs: "Image" Literature 8

Setting Goals 12

Timing 16

What To Talk About.............................32

The Sales Newsletter...........................35

The Employee Newsletter 44

The Customer Newsletter 53

Organization 62

Presentation 71

A Note to Freelance Writers 76

PREFACE

If the information presented here sounds like I know what I'm talking about (and I do hope it does) it's because I've written an awful lot of company newsletters in some twenty years in the advertising/publicity field and ten of those years as a freelance copywriter.

I'm still doing it, and still enjoying it, but I've turned down a lot of additional opportunities just because time will stretch only so far. If I can't do a good job for a client and give him all the time he requires, I'd rather he used someone who can.

You see, newsletter writing is a very personal service: your clients become personal friends, and you'll tend to become as involved in their business as if it were your own. You'll learn to hate their competitors, rejoice in their successes and worry over their problems. For that reason, I never work for two clients in the same business -- I'm a one-company woman! Besides, it would be unethical, since I'm often privy to advance intelligence or company secrets as a result of writing about them before they happen.

Of course, that's part of the fun -- and it is fun, as well as being highly profitable for the writer. I wish more writers would take on the job; there are so many companies in every city who could benefit from a newsletter or two of their own.

Perhaps, once you've read this book, you'll join me.

Gerene Reid

INTRODUCTION

Ever since Mr. Kiplinger began his insiders' report, everyone knows what a newsletter is.... there's at least one in print for every small segment of business, industry or career. But since this book is designed for freelance writers and others outside of the advertising/marketing field as well as those within it, perhaps not everyone knows what a <u>company</u> newsletter is.

I'll probably be telling some of you more than you really want to know throughout the book, so I may as well begin here: a company newsletter (or "house organ") is a communication from an officer or management group within a firm to a larger group which can be reached with a single publication. It may be from the Sales manager to the entire sales staff (whether salaried by the company or a group of individual sales firms such as manufacturers' sales representatives or distributors); from the Personnel manager or company President to all the employees; from company management to its customers; or possibly a combination of several groups.

A <u>company</u> newsletter differs from <u>trade</u> newsletters because it's strictly concerned with its own news and the goals it sets for the newsletter to accomplish. It deals with matters outside the company only when they are of specific interest to its readers. Company newsletters are written in-house (hence "house organ") by a member of the firm, by a writer from the company's advertising or public relations agency, or by a freelance writer working directly with the nominal "Editor" of the publication (the Sales manager, Personnel manager, etc.) or with the advertising agency.

Everyone agrees that company newsletters lift the morale of the employees, encourage the sales force and build goodwill among customers -- but everyone also seems to feel that writing a regular newsletter is a tremendous chore.... one that's better postponed indefinitely than begun.

They're right about the first consensus -- but the second one is all wet. Most of my freelance income is earned writing company newsletters, and if it really were drudgery, you can bet I wouldn't have continued it for over ten years!

If you enjoy talking to people, investigating new fields and finding better ways to say something on paper clearly and entertainingly, you can write your own newsletter, Mr. President or Sales Manager -- and have a lot of fun doing it.

Or, you can hire one of the freelance writers who is also reading this book and let him or her have the fun of doing it while you have the satisfaction of seeing it in print (with your name on it) and contemplating the tangible results!

The greatest advantage of hiring someone outside the company to handle the job is that they don't get paid till the issue is written, so you can be sure it will get done every month, or every quarter, or whatever period you decide on!

Even a very small company can have a newsletter (and should have at least a sales newsletter if it is using reps or distributors for a sales staff) since it can be done as inexpensively as the budget allows, and really can be written by almost anyone who's read this book. Even you.

Continue with me, and you'll see!

CHAPTER I

HOUSE ORGANS: "IMAGE" LITERATURE

The words you put into a company newsletter are called "copy", and copywriting is writing to sell something. House organs are a type of sales literature.... but they're much more subtle than an advertisement, which is considered "selling" literature or a catalog or data sheet which are "buying" literature.

Every piece of copy a company prints has some "sell"; some "buying" information; and some "image" in it. A company newsletter leans most heavily toward image. It's a very "soft-sell" salesman; it builds goodwill toward the company because it provides a service for its readers; by keeping them up-to-date, giving them new information, or perhaps even entertaining them. And, because they're favorably inclined toward the company for being so helpful, they're naturally going to be more inclined to buy its products, or to work harder on making or selling its products.

It may be going a long way around the barn, but it's a good back-up for the "hard-sell" ads, data sheets and personal selling the company is using to interest the customer and close the sale.

Like other types of "image" literature (annual reports, textbooks, etc.), the house organ or company newsletter has two goals. Its <u>apparent</u> goal is to provide information on products or selling techniques or happenings within the company; its <u>actual</u> goal is to influence its readers favorably toward the company....to give the company a favorable "image" in their minds.

In the case of a sales staff comprised of sales reps, for instance, the company's sales manager is dealing with a group of independent businessmen who sell other products than his....often many other products. He has no real control over the time and efforts of these people, as he might have with salaried salesmen. In fact, his only control is to fire them if they're not doing the job for him that he expects of them. To influence them, he can only persuade, not command. A regular sales newsletter keeps his company's name in front of these reps in a favorable manner....giving them helpful information.... so that hopefully they'll spend a greater portion of their time selling his product line.

It works. One of my clients has been publishing a bi-monthly sales newsletter for nine years. If an issue is held up in the mails, he gets immediate inquiries from his reps asking where it is. Better, his sales curve has risen steadily, even during recessions. And the newsletters are so informative that reps have kept them in looseleaf folders and give them to new salesmen to read as a sort of textbook.

Consistency is one of the chief advantages of a newsletter....and one of its greatest image-building attributes. When a customer sees a publication arriving every month in his mailbox, he begins to look forward to receiving it. Salesmen who've learned that there's helpful information in your company publication will take it home and read it when it arrives, and will anticipate its arrival. Employees check the company distribution points for the new issues a day or two before they are off the press.

<u>But skip an issue now and then, and the benefit of consistency is lost.</u> A newsletter that arrives now and again doesn't have a chance to become part of a reader's scheduled activity. It also assumes a haphazard image....and no one has real respect for a company that doesn't keep its own schedules.

In the reader's mind, that company probably won't keep its promises, either.

Another of my clients publishes a monthly newsletter for his customers, and at this writing he has never missed an issue in twelve years. (I'm really proud of him!). Each year he sends out a questionnaire asking customers' opinions of his products, services, etc. and asking them to specify if they want to continue receiving the newsletter. The mailing list....all requests.... has grown steadily every year. So has his business.

This client also publishes a monthly newsletter for his employees, and I've never known a company with better morale or more enthusiastic workers. His "image" with both groups is great!

NOTES

CHAPTER II

SETTING GOALS

While the "image" goals discussed in Chapter I are general, every newsletter has specific goals which must be kept in mind while you're researching and writing it....although they're usually very subtle and are implied rather than stated. These goals often influence the type of material you'll want to present in the newsletter and will definitely affect the way you slant your stories.

If you'll look over the following list of typical goals and the kinds of material that will help meet them, you'll notice that there are a number of overlaps. Because of this, it's possible to plan a newsletter to reach two or even all three of the audience groups.

Audience: Customers and Prospects

Goals

(A) Keep the company's name prominent
(B) Present a progressive company image
(C) Encourage inquiries
(D) Encourage loyalty to the company
(E) Educate the reader in company products

Subject Matter

(1) Product information
(2) Company news
(3) Application stories
(4) Personnel stories
(5) Ad reprints
(6) Design ideas
(7) Technical papers
(8) Offers of literature

Audience: Sales Force

Goals   Subject Matter

(A), (B), (D), (E)   (1), (2), (3), (4), (5), (6), (7)

(F) Educate the reader   (9) Sales techniques
    in special sales   (10) Sales figures
    techniques   (11) Company policies
                               (12) Sales success stories

Audience: Company Employees

Goals   Subject Matter

(B), (D), (E)   (1), (2), (3), (4), (5), (11)
(G) Present management
    views   (13) Safety, credit union,
(H) Promote participa-   other company program
    tion in company   news
    programs   (14) Employee news

    Of course, if you're trying to fit a publication to two groups, you'll present only information that's interesting to both audiences, so that a separate publication for each one can be tailored much more closely to your readers.

    For example, a company might publicize its sales figures to the sales force, but might not want to share them with its employees or its customers. Technical stories might or might not be over the head of employees; customers probably won't care if the Sales Manager has a new secretary; while the sales force isn't vitally interested in which production department had a perfect attendance record.

In short, the more people you try to reach with a single publication, the more complex your job becomes as you try to keep in mind all the people who'll read it, and select and slant material that will interest all the groups. On the other hand, if you publish a separate newsletter for each group, you can use much of the same material in two or all three of them, but still address your audience very personally with things that are of real interest to them.

As I'll point out in more detail, the same story can be "slanted" three different ways (or have three different emphases) and thus be tailored specifically for each of the three audience groups.

NOTES

CHAPTER III

TIMING

With the very first issue of a new publication you will need to know how often it will be published (monthly, quarterly, bi-monthly, etc.) and what the target publication date will be. You'll then have to determine how it will be produced, so that you can figure out how long it will take from initial interviews to final distribution.

A company publication can be anything from a 64-page, four-color "quarterly review" to a typewritten one-pager run off at the local "while-you-wait" offset printer's or the company's mimeo machine. You need to know, so you'll know when to get started.

Begin with the end of the publication cycle. Find out:

(1) How long it takes to get it in the mail (or in the company mailboxes) from the time the printer is finished with it.

(2) How long the printer will take from the time he gets "camera-ready art" till it's off his presses.

(3) How long it will take to get type set and the newsletter pasted up and ready for the printer.

(4) How long it will take to get all the necessary approvals on the copy from

the company officials who have to
initial it once it's written. (Sometimes
this can be the longest delay.)

(5) How long it will take to research, write
the newsletter, and deliver it to the
"Powers That Be" for approval. Remember
that on the first few go-rounds you'll
be spending extra time finding people
and establishing rapport and a working
system, so allow for it. Also allow a
few extra hours for collecting photos
or drawings to illustrate your stories..
..or for making drawings if you plan
to do your own illustrations. (More
about this later.) Admittedly, this
is all guestimate at this point, but try
to project as liberally as possible while
still remaining in the realm of possibil-
ity. As you get busier, you'll appreciate
any extra time allowances you've built
in at the beginning.

Researching

Depending upon the type of newsletter you're
writing and the subject matter it will contain, you may
be dealing with from one to twenty different people as
news "sources". (I'll go into specific types of newsletters later). With one monthly sales newsletter I
talk only with the Sales Manager of the company. With
another, for a different company, I contact everyone
from the President to the Chief Engineer. This is a
technical product line, and much of the product and

application details are not available from the sales department. In still another publication, this time to customers, I've never even met the client! I work entirely with the Account Executive at the company's advertising agency, and he deals with the client.

In every case, though, there has to be one "key" person who'll decide what will be in the issue. Usually he'll be shown on the newsletter masthead as the Editor of the publication....though that's not necessarily the case. In one of my sales newsletters the Marketing Manager was shown as the Editor, while the Sales Manager actually did the work. Determine who the "key contact" will be, and start with him each time. Then, if you have others to visit, he'll know in advance who they are and will probably clear the way for you or steer you to the right people.

Be Businesslike

While an "outside" writer coming in each month or each quarter or whenever the publishing period is should certainly plan ahead and make appointments for interviews, it may be even more important for an "inside" writer to follow the same procedure. Unless you're the president of the company, people seem to feel no compunction about brushing you off, interrupting your interviews or postponing your visits if you're "one of them".

I learned this, to my dismay, when I accepted a temporary job as ad director for a company which had been my freelance client, until they located a permanent ad manager. No sooner had I been established at a desk in their building than the sales people and engineers I had to use as key sources for the newsletter became suddenly and mysteriously invisible.....or at least incredibly slippery! Oddly enough, once I went back to being an "outsider" some three months later, they were once again accessible!

So, do your homework for each publication period, whether you're an insider or an outsider:

(1) Make an appointment with your key contact at least a week in advance. Set a time as well as a date, and confirm it the day before.

(2) Ask your key contact or his secretary to make appointments for you with the other people in the company you'll have to see that day, so you can do the whole thing in one trip. Or, make the supplementary appointments yourself, spacing them out according to the time you expect each interview to take, or when your contacts are available. It may take extra time to set up your day this way, but it will take a lot more time if you have to make several trips.

(3) Be on time for your appointment....even a bit early, if possible. When your contacts know you'll be there when you say you will, they'll keep open the time you need.

(4) Know ahead of time what you're going to talk about with each contact, and get right to it. Take as little of his time as possible; he'll appreciate it and be more willing to spend time with you next time around. It also saves your time, which becomes increasingly valuable as

you get busier. If your contact likes to shoot the breeze, try to get the business part of the interview over with first.

(5) No matter what your regular job, if you're an "insider", present a businesslike appearance for your newsletter interviews. To this contact, at this time, you're a newsletter editor, not a welder or typist, or whatever your regular job is, so dress like a newsletter editor. If you're an "outsider", remember that business people are innately suspicious of "advertising types", and have a mental image of jeans and sweatshirts, untrimmed beards, bare feet and a habit of exaggeration. You're going to have to relate to these people and develop a good working relationship, so give the impression that you're one of them....even if you normally do work in jeans and sweatshirts. Dress as they do and adopt their attitudes..... temporarily. Otherwise they're liable to freeze up and waste your time as you struggle to get through the barrier. (Engineers, in particular, are firmly convinced that anything they say is likely to be exaggerated in print, and they'll get hung with it. Do your best to set them at ease.)

(6) Try to handle only one publication research visit in a single day. When you're working with a number of different companies, you'll find you're liable to get confused if you research one company's newsletter in the morning and a different one in the afternoon.

Since you're temporarily an "insider" when you

are writing the newsletter, a contact may be offended if you forget that his sales people are reps, not salaried (as are the salesmen in the company you researched that morning), and he'll soon lose respect for your memory....if not your basic intelligence....if you make too many mistakes of that sort. For that day, you are a member of his company, and he wants (and deserves) all of your attention to his publication.

Even if your research takes only half a day, scurry back to the typewriter for the rest of the day and work on that publication rather than trying to save some mileage on the old Pontiac and seeing a whole different group of people in the afternoon.

(7) If you're doing several publications for the same company, it will save time to research more than one in the same visit, but keep firmly in mind which newsletter you're working on with each contact, and what its goals are. Otherwise, you're liable to ask the wrong questions or get the wrong slant on a story (which will confuse your contact during the interview, and will confuse you when you try to write the story).

Taking Notes

If at all possible, carry a small tape recorder with you on your research visits. Frantically trying to take notes when people are talking can absorb all your attention, so that you don't really hear what they're saying. If you're secure in the knowledge that the recorder is getting all the words (and please do check it at the beginning of each conversation. Playing back a blank tape when you're ready to write can be a disastrous experience!), you can concentrate on what your interviewee is saying, ask for clarification where necessary, pose new questions....in short, get all the facts.

If you're just scribbling down what he wants to tell you, you're bound to have some weak spots in your story, since he doesn't always think along the same lines as you, and he doesn't really know what you're after. You, after all, have to reorganize what he says and put it in writing so other people can understand it. It's amazing how disjointed a casual conversation can be, so make sure <u>one</u> of you stays on the track.

I learned the real advantage of the tape recorder when I was still back in the take-notes-by-shorthand-and-scribble period. After my research visit I set my notebook on the roof of the car while I was stowing stuff away; forgot it; and drove off into the sunset, strewing precious scrawls all over the countryside! Doing a newsletter entirely from memory is an experience I'd only want <u>once</u>. (I hang the tape recorder around my neck, by the way, so it won't be a victim of my absent-mindedness.)

During the interview I generally take notes of the key points made while the tape recorder is running. It helps me to keep track of what's been said ....and what <u>hasn't</u> yet been said; to make note of printed material given to me as supplementary source material; to record suggestions on whom to see about certain points that need clarifying or additional data;

and to know where on the tape certain information is recorded. Since I may not want to transcribe the entire tape(s) before I start writing the newsletter, the notes help me find the data I need for each story ....another valuable time-saver.

Getting The Facts

(1) Most people get very shy when they realize that what they're talking about is liable to end up in print....especially when you're using a tape recorder.....so the first thing to do on your initial visit with a contact is to set him at ease. Assure him that the reason for the tape recorder is strictly to allow you to give him your entire attention, and that no one will hear the tape but you, when you transcribe it. (Since Watergate I've noticed this tendency to freeze in front of a recorder has become even more widespread!).

Assure your contact, also, that he'll have a chance to review the manuscript before it goes to print, so that he can make any "improvements" he feels necessary. Then make sure your primary contact does submit the material to the person who gave you the material. To make doubly sure, send a copy of that story only to your interviewee and ask him to give your primary contact any changes.

(2) If you're planning to use basically the same story in two of the company's newsletters, decide in advance just how you'll present it to each of the two audiences, so you'll be sure to

get all the necessary facts from your contact for each version of the story.

For example, a progressive new piece of equipment may be a good story for both a customer newsletter and one to employees. In the customer newsletter you'll want to play up the <u>benefits to the customer</u>, i.e., NEW WELDING POSITIONER SPEEDS PRODUCTION, CUTS DELIVERY TIME. You'll want to get specifics such as a percentage of time saved with the new equipment, how many days sooner the company can now promise delivery, how much more accurate the welds will be with the new positioner, how the new equipment fits into an overall plan of streamlining production in your progressive, forward-looking company, etc.

In the employee newsletter you'll want to give some background on how the company came to select this equipment, what it does for the flow of materials in the plant, <u>who</u> will be operating it, <u>who</u> was responsible for choosing the equipment, when other employees can see it in operation, etc. In cases where new equipment implies a step toward that bad word, "automation", the key to your story may be reassuring employees that the new equipment does not mean lost jobs. JOE PETERSON HAS A NEW, BIGGER JOB, is a possible headline (with a picture of Joe and the Marvelous Machine), or NEW SKILLS FOR OUR WELDERS, implying that our welders are not losing their jobs, but learning to do them better.

(3) Discuss with your contact what the story will be about and what the slant will be so that he'll know the kinds of information you need. When he understands what you're after, he may come up with a new slant that's even better than the ones you had in mind. But get all the facts.... even some you may not use in the final version of your story. It's much better to have too much information and have to cut your story than to try to fill empty space from an empty cupboard. And coming back to your contact later for data you neglected to get the first time around can completely blow your professional image.

Illustrations

A picture may not be worth a thousand words (in fact, as a writer I'll fight that concept to the death!) but it certainly helps to make your stories appear more interesting, and an illustration will always be an attention-getter.

In most cases a photograph (or, in buzz-word language, a "half-tone") is most useful in a newsletter. When you're discussing each story with your contacts, see if there's a glossy photo available of the machine, person, etc. you're writing about, or if the company can arrange to take one.

This is probably the spot for a briefing that many of you probably won't need. An illustration that's drawn (ink or very black pencil on white paper) is called a "line drawing" or "line art." This can include cartoons, charts, etc. that are photographed by the printer's camera exactly the way type is photographed. It's a single tone....all black.

Photographs have a variety of tones....whites, shades of gray and even shades of black....which the camera cannot pick up satisfactorily. In order to print them, they must be "screened", or photographed through a "screen" which contains many tiny dots. The photo produced by screening is made up of black dots..... clustered thickly together where the dark tones appear and spaced out where the lighter ones are....so that they can be printed as line art.

Glossy black-and-white photos reproduce most satisfactorily, even those you may do yourself with a standard camera or Polaroid. You can use color photos, however, if there's a great deal of contrast between the lights and darks. Color photos that are all pretty much the same tone range will print very muddily, and with little detail. I often use a Polaroid with an attached screen that produces a photo already screened for the printer's use. (Available through Ed Grant, P.O. Box 56, Bloomingville, OH 43152.) If time allows and the client's budget permits, however, I prefer to use a good 35 mm. camera with black-and-white film (usually Tri-X for indoor shots with available light) and have the lab make contact prints for me so I can choose the one I want to use. Then I let the printer do the screening.

Whether you're taking photos yourself or directing another photographer, try to get a little extra interest into the shot. Mr. Boss handing a five-year pin to Ms. Employee isn't going to catch many eyes...except Ms. Employee's and her family's....but an unusual angle or some evident emotion in the photo may help. A picture of a machine standing still is dull; but the machine in operation, possibly with some blurring to show movement, has some interest. I once took a long shot down an empty hallway when a plant was being remodeled, and the perspective, with all lines converging to a tiny little painter at the end of the hall, made a surprisingly artistic picture.

Next to photos, charts and graphs are effective illustrations. People would rather look at a bar chart showing the company's sales over the past five years than read the figures....though the figures should also be in the story.

And, while photos and charts help to tell your story, sometimes you'll want line illustrations (pen-and ink drawings) just to make the overall appearance of the newsletter more attractive. There are several "clip art" services which provide glossy black-on-white illustrations you can use, the company may have some artists on the payroll, or you may be able to do your own. Often full-service printers have clip-art available for you to use, too.

While you're discussing each story with your contact, think about possible illustrations and ask him about them. If photos are already available, get a copy on the spot so you can plan for it. Remember, too, to allow for space for the illustrations in the organizer you prepare to submit with your copy.

With a newsletter, though, illustrations are an adjunct to the story. Don't use them for a crutch. What you say and how you say it is the most important factor.

From that, you can decide <u>when</u> you'll have to do your research. Some examples:

(A) One employee newsletter is scheduled for distribution on the fifteenth of each month. It takes 3 days for the "quickie" printer to run it and deliver it, and it's distributed inhouse that same day. It takes 2 days for the approved copy to be typeset and about 4 days for the material I submit to be approved and any necessary rewrite done. Research takes me half a day, and writing about one day....though this can be shortened by working in the evening, over a weekend, etc.

That's a total of ten or eleven days, so I try to set my research visits for the first of the month, or as close to it as possible.

(B) A customer four-page newsletter is produced by the advertising agency. Since it's a fancier job than the above, both in production and in printing, it takes 2 weeks for the printer and 3 days for the mailing. Another 2 weeks is spent in production while the agency has type set, collects illustrations and prepares camera-ready art. The client generally takes another week to approve the copy and layout, and the research and writing take three days.

Fortunately this is a quarterly publication, which is mailed on the first of the month, so to make sure I have some leeway on the 41 days required, I generally start my research six weeks in advance of the publication date. For the July first issue, then, I begin researching about May fifteenth.

You'll often find that after a newsletter is under way, <u>you're</u> the only one vitally concerned with the deadline, so you'll have to take the initiative in getting each issue started on time. Don't be tempted to let it slide; if issues start to slip beyond dealine, one of two unhappy results can be expected: an issue will be skipped, and once that's happened, it can happen again....and again; or, the company will simply give up the whole idea, since it can't be kept up without a lot of hassle. And so, another promising communication bites the dust.

As I've said before, a newsletter's chief value is in its consistency. <u>That responsibility belongs to the writer</u>. Coax, persuade or bulldoze, but <u>get the newsletter started on time</u> so it has a fighting chance of getting published on time.

Once you've determined that your starting date should be on the first of the month (or the tenth, or whenever), <u>inform your contacts</u> so they can start collecting items for the newsletter during the month and have them ready for you when you call on them. You'll still make specific appointments, if possible, but they'll know in advance that you'll be around close to the first of each month.

<u>Plan Ahead</u>

Once you've done the initial issue of a newsletter, you'll have an idea of its normal content and can list possible subjects before you call on your contacts. It often helps to fill in the holes when the contact runs dry of ideas (and some of them <u>start out</u> dry), and it provides a foundation to build on.

If, for example, you're researching the February issue and your contact mentions there will be a new product announcement in April, make note of it and stick it on your list of things to ask him about for the April issue. If you're doing personnel "profiles" each month, get a list in advance of possible people to feature for the next several months. Think of possible stories of interest to your readers for the future....the new test lab, a new price schedule, an explanation of the employees' suggestion system, a running report on the credit union, some applications stories that may be coming up shortly.

Even if you're not naturally nosey (I am), you're bound to pick up ideas for other issues on each research visit. Jot them down in advance. It will impress your contacts with your personal interest and judicious planning, and it will fill a lot of blank space in the newsletter. After you've been writing to come up with practically the whole issue all by yourself....and that will be a tremendous relief to a contact who consistently stares woefully across his desk at you and says, "I can't think of anything to talk about." Once you get him going with your own list, he comes up with a <u>lot</u> of good material!

NOTES

CHAPTER IV

WHAT TO TALK ABOUT

What you say in a newsletter depends on two factors: who's writing it and who's reading it. For that discussion, we'll have to take each type of newsletter separately.

Since every writer, insider or outsider, will identify with the company he's writing for, I refer to "your company" in the stuff that follows. If you are a free-lance writer, translate that to "your client's company".

Also, with today's exaggerated insistence on the use of "person" instead of words denoting gender, let me absolve myself for the whole book by explaining that when I refer to "chairman", it can mean either man or woman, while "him" can also be "her". (I was probably born "emancipated", since I've never felt the need for further "liberation", but for those of you who are sensitive to sex subtleties in print, I apologize. The habits of years are hard to break, and "him or her" takes up a lot of space when you use it over and over.)

Since I can't find another suitable spot for this comment in the book, let me also mention here that being a woman in this business has never been a problem for me, although until recently I've dealt almost exclusively with men in business. If you are obivously competent in what you do, and obviously (even exaggeratedly) interested in what your contact does, it won't matter to him (or her, darn it!) whether you're male, female or indeterminate. Everyone likes to be an expert, and if you can make your contact feel like an authority and appear a hero to his fellow-workers and his management, you'll establish rapport without regard to sex.

<u>Choosing   A Name</u>

If you're starting a brand-new newsletter, you should help your company come up with a catchy name for it. Some firms ask for help from employees or customers, as in a contest, but most of them will depend on you. Try to come up with three of four so they have a choice.

The best approach to a name is some sort of tie-in with the company's product, its name, or the occupation of the readers. PURCHASING PULSE is one newsletter I write for a client's customers who are purchasing people. A sales newsletter for a company whose initials were K.W. was named "Know-ho<u>W</u>". Another sales newsletter for Digitran Company <u>was</u> called "Digihear?" Union Federal Savings & Loan calls its customer newsletter STATE OF THE UNION, while a mutual savings bank client of mine chose MUTUAL INTEREST. An employee newsletter for a distributor (which handles many product lines) is called "Between The Lines". "Seals-Talk" is printed by a plastic-seal manufacturer.

The possibilities are endless, so make a long list and then pick out the ones you like best to submit. If you give a client too many choices, he'll find it hard to make a decision....and you <u>don't</u> want the first issue held up while everyone argues <u>about</u> what to call it!

NOTES

CHAPTER V

THE SALES NEWSLETTER

Normally this is a monthly publication, since salesmen....especially reps or distributors....have short memories, and it's important to keep your company's name prominent in their minds with frequent communications. You might go to a bi-monthly when you're regularly in contact with them through other means, such as correspondence and daily phone calls, but any longer period than bi-monthly won't accomplish much.

Tone

A sales newsletter is generally "Edited" by the Marketing Manager, Sales Manager, V.P. Sales, or other sales management person, and it's generally pretty personal. Try to really listen to the Editor and pick up his speech mannerisms, favorite expressions, etc., so that you can make the newsletter sound as if he actually had written it. Because the newsletter is "just between us sales types" it can be light in tone, use slang expressions, cartoons, and generally sound conversational and "insider-oriented". (They're really the most fun to do, because salesmen are extroverted people and easy to talk to.)

Here's an example: a paragraph from one of my sales newsletters. "We've been running close to capacity this last year; business has been good and is getting better still. You're probably aware that our production time for dipped radials, particularly, has dropped from 16 weeks to about 10 weeks. However, by January first we can start really producing; the bottlenecks will be worked out; all our new equipment will be on-line; and we'll have a production capacity 2 or 3 times greater than the past year."

It's newsy and easy-reading, but still literate. Don't fall into the trap of using self-conscious slang though, such as "now us folks can really start producin' fer you-all". It sounds silly and will offend most readers. (One popular magazine does this consistently, and I'm about to end my subscription, even though the content is of tremendous interest to me.)

Content

Salesmen are interested in anything that will help them close a sale....from how to set up their own biorhythm chart (or their customers') to a new application for your product that may open up a new group of prospects for them.

Since the sales newsletter is published frequently, you can set up regular features, such as a "Rep of the Month"....a "profile" of a different sales rep company each month, telling what his regional market is like, how he started in the business, who his salesmen are, what complementary lines he carries, what applications he most frequently finds for your products, etc. This is generally a popular feature, since people like to see their names in print, and a profile can be researched in a fifteen-minute phone call if you prepare your questions ahead of time.

Another regular feature can be a message from

the Sales Manager on a particular sales problem, product advantage, etc. You might also have a company profile of a different person each month who deals with the sales force or whose work is indirectly of interest to them, i.e., the Chief Engineer talking about upcoming new products; the Accounting head talking about how commissions are determined; the Production Manager discussing why a product is made a certain way.

A popular feature is "gossip" around the territories: what rep has added new salesmen; what salesman just fathered twins; who carried off a sizeable order. Success stories of salesmen's more "creative" sales always interest other salesmen, and they're usually receptive to helpful hints about selling techniques <u>as long as you don't talk down to them</u>. Treat the suggestion as a "reminder" of something they already know, but never presume to <u>teach</u> them anything about selling! They'll feel (and probably rightly so) that they know more about selling than you'll ever learn, and they'll resent your presumption.

The most important content of the newsletter must be information about your company's products: what new ones are coming up; how to use the ones now on the production line; what changes you're making in current products; how to meet objections from customers; what the competition is doing and how to combat it; how different customer companies are using your products (in what specific applications) and how they're benefiting.

It doesn't do a salesman any good to learn that the finish on a new product is "matte black" unless he can use the information to <u>sell</u>. Are there any other

37

color options? Do they cost more? Was the matte black finish chosen for a special reason, such as being heat-absorbent? Even if it's only offered in matte black because that's the only color you can <u>make</u> it in, present it as "the <u>popular</u> matte black finish". He can pick up on that to persuade his customers that everyone else is selecting matte black because of its more attractive appearance, so that's why it's the best color.

This is the kind of stuff that helps a salesman sell, and if he's working on commission, especially, it's what he is looking for in your newsletter.

If your product line is really technical, it will help to know the company's Chief Engineer, Applications Engineers and anyone else who can translate "engineering-ese" into English for you. Some technical companies' salesmen are all engineers, but most of them are salesmen first and technical types second, so talk to them in straightforward language. Explain the technical terms (prefacing it with something like: "<u>As you know</u>, ambient noise is the interference of stray signals....") and <u>always</u> talk about your subject with how-to-sell-it in mind.

Here's one approach I used: give the salesman the information so he can educate the customer (and, secretly, educate himself).

"To really communicate with a customer, you have to be sure you're both on the same wavelength. If he's new to buying capacitors, your knowledgeable spouting of 'dielectric constants' or 'dissipation factor' will be so much gibberish to him. Sometimes basic education is in order.

"To start from scratch, a capacitor is a component that stores an electrical charge. Essentially, it consists of two conductor surfaces separated by an insulator or 'dielectric'. The largest charge that the dielectric can store is determined by two factors: (1) the dielectric constant of that insulator material (which varies with temperature); and (2) the highest voltage that can be placed across the conductive surfaces without rupturing the dielectric......etc."

It might be helpful for you if I give you some examples of content in sales newsletters I've done:

Page 1: THE "WHY'S" OF THE COMPANY'S GROWTH
(A review of the marketplace for the company's products, their share-of-market, and where to look for sales.)

SHOWTIME!
(Recap of a recent Trade Show, with a photo of the company's booth. Emphasis was on questions asked by customers.)

Page 2: THE VEEPEE IS A LADY
(Profile of a company officer)

BEYOND OUR BORDERS
(Update on foreign sales)

OUR NEW COMPUTER IS BUSINESS-ORIENTED
(How the new computer system affects the sales force, i.e., processing orders, commission checks, etc.)

Page 3: VIEWPOINT
(A discussion of Quality Control by the Q.C. Manager.)

BITS AND PIECES
(Local "gossip": new rep organization, visitors to the plant; congratulations to another rep organization for record sales during past month; new inside people added to company's sales staff.)

TIMELY TECHNICAL TIPS
(A review of information contained in the company's catalog, pointing out special points of information, by the company's marketing engineer.)

Page 4: SALES-TALK
(Regular column by the Sales Manager, this one dealing with how to sell a specific product line.)

PROFILE
(An outline of one of the company's sales rep organizations, with the principal officer suggesting that reps call more on Manufacturing Engineers.)

Here's another, for a different company:

Page 1: TOUCH AND TELL
(Describing a new application for one of the company's products.)

WHAT'S UP DOWN UNDER
> (Another application, this time from Australia.)

THE FIRST QUARTER WAS A GOOD ONE
> (A recap of sales figures for the first three months, showing how each rep company stands relative to the others.)

Page 2: A NEW PERSPECTIVE
> (Review of the company's new advertising strategy.)

NEW PROBLEM SOLVERS
> (Introduction (with photos) of two new management people.)

ROUNDTABLE
> (Comments by several rep organization presidents on their respective markets, competitors, sales techniques, new applications and individual promotion. Written as a conversation between them, I got my input by sending each of them a detailed questionaire with lots of space for them to answer, and a self-addressed, stamped envelope. This became a monthly feature.)

Page 3: BOB IS A BULLDOG
> (Profile of the Marketing Manager.)

FIRST YOU HAVE TO GET THEIR ATTENTION
> (Quote from an article in a sales maga-

zine about making up to five calls on
the same prospect.)

SMALLER IS NOT ALWAYS BETTER
(Comment on a competitor's product,
why their own is better, and how to
sell the advantages.)

Page 4: MEDICAL ELECTRONICS IS THE BIG COMER
(Discussion of a new market for the
company's products and suggestions
for getting in on it.)

WE NEED YOUR HELP
(Request for market data from the field,
with a printed coupon for the reps to
fill out and return.)

NEED A FEW MORE RIGHT HANDS?
(How reps can work with distributors to
the benefit of both.)

Contacts

The number of contacts you'll be talking to will differ with the company and the philosophy of the newsletter's Editor. With one of my clients, I talk only with the Sales Manager, though he'll steer me to Engineering in special cases. With another client's sales newsletter I cover a regular "beat", talking to engineers, marketing people, product managers, the distributor sales manager and the regional sales managers as well as my key contact.

NOTES

CHAPTER VI

THE EMPLOYEE NEWSLETTER

While the salesman's major interest is his business .... selling.... the employee newsletter gets much more personal. If a salesman sells more, the company benefits. But for the company to benefit from all its employees, it must encourage more production, less time off, less tardiness and a company "esprit de corps" that will motivate the employees to feel a part of the company and be willing to give it their extra effort.

The employee newsletter can be a sensitive communication... particularly if the company's image with its employees isn't awfully favorable when you begin the newsletter. But a newsletter can do a lot to help a situation like that, just by showing them that management is interested enough in them to make this effort.... to communicate, to ask for their feedback, to keep them informed instead of relying on rumors, and to let them know that the Front Office really is made up of live, approachable human beings.

Tone

For that reason, I'm in favor of a chatty, light tone, very conversational, instead of a formal newspaper style. If the Personnel Manager or President is going to be the Editor, try to adopt his personal speech mannerisms (unless they're stiff and formal. In that case, "improve" upon them).

Actually, one of the most successful of my

employee newsletters has no editor's name on the masthead. It's been published regularly every month for eleven years; the key contact has changed four or five times; even the writer has been changed a couple of times (when I was on vacation); and no one has ever been the wiser. The conversational tone is easy to copy, and the research trips have turned into a regular regimen. In the space of two or three hours I talk with five management people and six "stringers" (employees who volunteer to collect personal items from their departments throughout the month and turn them over to me on my visit), then take my tapes and notes back to the typewriter and <u>do</u> it.

Having no nominal "Editor" is often an advantage, since the employee newsletter is the voice of management, and if there's an unpopular point to put across, no one management person has to take the kickback from it. (Sometimes <u>I</u> do, though!)

Here's a paragraph from that publication:

"Calling all golfers! Only <u>one</u> person has signed up for our Duffers' Tournament since last month. You must have forgotten to <u>call Roger Brown on extension 228</u>. Now's the time to learn to play golf..or practice up (and golf is a <u>very</u> 'in' game, just now.) Take advantage of this opportunity by telling Roger you'd like to swing a club...or dig a divot...or whatever."

<u>Content</u>

Employees <u>are</u> interested in their company.... and remember that "employee" includes everyone from a design engineer to the janitor, so don't decide your reader is some dumb machine operator and start being patronizing. As a matter of fact, most of the machine operators I know are bright, interesting people. They're as concerned with the company's progress as are its stockholders, and as interested in its new products as is the sales force.

But their interest isn't in how to sell the product or how the customer benefits from it, but <u>who</u> designed it, <u>who</u> made the prototype, <u>who's</u> lead man on the new production line. They like to see their names in print (don't we all?), so give them lots of names. Stringers are especially valuable in preparing a company newsletter, since employees know their fellow employees better than you or I, or even their management can. A "personal" column is very popular in this type of newsletter, talking about who got promoted, had her fifteenth grandchild, celebrated a 25th wedding anniversary, welcomed a first child, graduated from a training course, is recovering from an operation, etc. Try not to get caught up in who-went-where for vacation, though. <u>Everyone</u> takes a vacation, and you may end up with inspiring items like: "Jimmy Jones of Production Control had a lot of fun working in his garden for two weeks".

Profiles of other employees are of real interest, too, but don't start with the president and work down. Mix in some of the lesser-status people, as well. One good way is to start with the oldest employee (in seniority) and work backward from there. Put some personal things in, like what their hobbies are, how many grandchildren they may have, and so on.

Another important area is exciting applications for the company's products. You'll be surprised at how interested....and proud....most employees are to learn that the products they helped to build were in a Moon Flight or in Detroit's newest sexmobile, or helping to conserve energy, or whatever. And since most of them don't read the magazines where your company advertises, reprint your latest ads for them, as well as new product releases or newspaper clippings where the company's name is mentioned. (If your advertising department doesn't have a file of these, it <u>should</u>.)

They're interested in what the company is doing to make their jobs safer, more interesting or pleasanter. If the cafeteria's going to be remodeled, tell them in advance. Talk up the Credit Union or the Scholarship Fund, and give the names of the departmental Safety Stewards. Give the results of the safety contest or Zero-Defects programs.

The employee newsletter is also a place to prepare people for upcoming changes and reassure them so that they don't get caught up in a vicious rumor-cycle. If you're planning to put in a new computer system, tell them well before you start. Explain the benefits to <u>them</u>, and tell them what inconveniences might result while the new Brain is being debugged. A lot of poor employee morale can be avoided by keeping people in the know.

And if there's an unpleasant subject to be discussed, don't avoid it. Be straightforward: tell them why it happened; why the decision was made; and what the results will likely be. They'll respect their management for being honest, and with facts to think about instead of rumors to worry about, they'll act rationally.

I've often been amazed at the apprehension some management people exhibit about the attitude of their own employees. Working both sides of the Front Office, as I do, I've been able to see how each group underestimates and misunderstands the other. A good employee newsletter can forestall a lot of this distrust.

Here's the content of some actual employee newsletters I've published. In most cases they're informal, without structured paging, so I'll just list them for you without giving pages numbers.

> HAVE YOU EVER WONDERED...
> (A complete "tour" -- with photos -- of the company's production line.)
>
> WE WELCOME:
> (List of new employees and departments.)
>
> MARY'S CATCHING UP!
> ("Profile" of a Lead Girl on Assembly.)
>
> SPEAKING OF INSURANCE
> (Check your dependent coverage if both spouses are working. You may be paying for more coverage than you can collect.)
>
> PETE HONEYWELL RETIRES
> (Photo of President making gift award, picture of retirement party.)

INSIDE ITEMS
    (Gossip: marriages, promotions, softball and bowling results, plans for company picnic, etc.)

WE'RE "SUPPLIER OF THE YEAR"
    (Story with picture of an award made to company by one of its customers.)

THE MOST DANGEROUS SPORT...
    (Humorous tale about several minor injuries to employees playing cricket.)

Another issue included:

OUR NUCLEAR PRODUCTS BUSINESS GROWS
    (New orders in-house for products for nuclear power plants.)

CLOTHES MAY NOT MAKE THE PERSON...
    (Safety article on dangerous articles of clothing.)

TELEPHONES MEAN BUSINESS
    (Don't use them for personal calls.)

MEET ED MATTHEWS
    (Profile of a management person.)

LOCALS:
    (Gossip, similar to above.)

NOW WE'RE FORTY
    (Brief history of the company.)

NEW RESPONSIBILITIES
   (Recap of several promotions for employees.)

WE'LL BE ON MINUTEMAN
   (Exciting application for company products.)

SCORES...SCORES...SCORES
   (Update on bowling and softball league standings.)

WE CONGRATULATE OUR "OLD TIMERS"
   (Award of service pins.)

SAUERKRAUT, ANYONE?
   (Discount tickets available to employees for local tourist attractions.)

LONGER DAYS, SHORTER WEEKS
   (Proposed new hours for all employees.)

Contacts

In the employee newsletter more than any other a variety of contacts is important. I've already mentioned "stringers". Try to get department heads to help you set up a regular list, and then talk to each of your "company reporters" about the kind of information you'd like them to collect. Generally there's a person in each department (or one for several departments) who's outgoing and enjoys doing this sort of thing. Then visit them on each research trip and pick their material. Make sure they understand that you may not use every item they supply (because of "company policy") so you won't get caught in the "vacation syndrome", and assure them that they don't have to write it themselves, just get you the facts.

While you'll start with your key contact, you should also check with the sales and advertising departments, the engineering department and other groups which might contribute items of general interest to the whole employee roster. Clear this with your key contact first, though....don't just go wandering through the plant on your own. You're liable to be ungraciously escorted <u>out</u> by the security people.

NOTES

CHAPTER VII

THE CUSTOMER NEWSLETTER

Only a little less sensitive than the employee newsletter is the one directed to customers: here "image" is of paramount importance. While a typewritten "quickie" appearance is fine for insiders like the sales force and employees (in fact, probably even better than a "slick" appearance, since it's more personal), a customer sees your newsletter as a representative of your company. If you send him an obviously cheap and hastily-written publication, it's like visiting him in dirty jeans and sneakers...he will not be impressed with your success, business acumen or financial stability. And he wants to do business with people who have (or at least appear to have) all these things.

That doesn't mean the newsletter has to be prohibitively expensive. If you're on a very tight budget, a two-page (front and back of one sheet) newsletter is fine....just have it typeset (with today's "cold-set" processes such as MT/SC and Compugraphics, it's not expensive to have this done), and print it on a nice-looking masthead. For an extra touch, have your mastheads printed in advance in a colored ink (you can do this in large volume to save money) and then have each issue printed in black on the pre-printed masthead.

A newspaper format is very suitable for a customer newsletter, and as money allows you can make it "slicker". One of my clients publishes a quarterly report with some 16 pages and a four-color cover.

Another does a 4-page quarterly newspaper. They both do an excellent job, because once the printed "salesman" is in the door, looking neat and alert, what counts is <u>what he says</u>. So, with as presentable an appearance as you can afford, the most important aspect of the customer newsletter is its content.

<u>Tone</u>

In tone, a customer newsletter is more objective than either of the other two, and more formal. It seldom has a masthead "editor", since the company itself is nominally the editor; and because a whole company is writing, there's no flavor of any one individual in the tone.

A newspaper approach is best, using the editorial "we" -- but don't get caught up in the "alleges" and "he affirmed" or other stilted phrases of which newspaper writers are so enamored. "More formal" simply means avoid slang expressions unless they are part of a quote. Go ahead and use contractions and keep the tone conversational, but not chatty. Make it as easy to read as you can, so the customer will read as much of it as possible.

As an example of tone, the following paragraph was used in a savings and loan association's customer newsletter:

"While we seem to be moving rapidly toward a 'paper society', a checkbook is really excess baggage for a lot of people. A practical person who writes only a few checks a month doesn't need to keep even a small part of his money tied up in the minimum balance required by a checking account. Instead of paying checking account service charges with his money, he can keep it earning interest in a passbook account."

Content

Here, more than in any other newsletter, your objective will be to sell, but so subtly that your reader hardly suspects it. All the stories are slanted to emphasize benefits to the customer. In that story about the new product, for example, the point to make in the customer newsletter is how it will enhance the customer's product or life, particularly if it's "the only", "the first", or "the best" on the market.

If it's a very competitive product, understand your company's philosophy about dealing with the competition. Some people have stuck with the old (and usually more acceptable) custom of referring to "Brand X", while others go ahead and name their competitors. Frankly, I think it's a mistake to call out a competitor's name. Why give him free publicity in your newsletter? And some customers may be completely turned off if you try to sell by knocking the competition.

Customers are interested in the key personnel in your organization -- particularly those with whom they deal personally, such as your sales staff, top management, etc., so company personnel profiles on such people are a good item to use. So are regular columns from the company president or top management people, as long as they deal with problem solving, forecasts, or some other subject of personal interest to the customer.

New products, new applications for old products, case histories, even items of general interest to your industry with appropriate comments or "editorializing" from one of your management people are always of interest to your customers. New management people should be introduced in the newsletter. New equipment or processes (as long as they stress customer benefits, such as faster delivery), new company policies and new services available to customers are always good material.

If your company is cited with an award from a customer, publicize it in the newsletter, but be sure to accompany it with a "thank you" to the citing customer....and don't add any words of praise to yourself. Be modest and appreciative without blowing your own horn. Reprint copies of your ads, too, in case customers missed them.

If you want feedback from the customers, offer them copies of current literature and print an order blank in the newsletter or enclose a separate one. You can also reprint speeches or technical papers presented by your people and offer them to customers. If you have a slide presentation or some other special service available, offer it to them in the newsletter and make it easy for them to ask for it, either by means of your order coupon or by giving them a toll-free phone number to call. In short, put into the newsletter anything that will benefit the customer by informing him, enhancing his status in his company, saving him money, or making his life easier and pleasanter.

Here are the stories contained in the savings & loan's newsletter for one issue:

Page 1: TWO EASY WAYS TO EARN MORE MONEY
(Certificates of deposit and how they work. Introducing two new ones.)

BOTH A BORROWER AND A LENDER BE
(Borrowing on your savings accounts.)

Page 2: UN-CONFUSING INTEREST
(Explaining terms like "compounding", "yield", etc.)

THE "MINIMUM" IS JUST FOR STARTERS
(Explaining more bank terms.)

MINIATURE LANDSCAPES FOR WINTER GREENERY
(An educational piece on container gardening.)

Page 3: WHY ARE BANKS SO NOSEY?
(The questions you're asked when you apply for a loan, and why banks ask them.)

INFLATION-FIGHTING TIPS
(Another non-banky story giving ideas for recycling items, etc.)

ARE YOU ON OUR MAILING LIST?
(Coupon to get your name on the M.L.)

SUPER NEW ACCOUNT
(A new offering by the bank to customers.)

Page 4:   CHALLENGER
            (Crossword puzzle incorporating bank terms or slogans. This one has "Higher Interest" worked into it.)

          CONGRATULATIONS, LYNDA
            (Bank officer named to Governor's commission.)

          IRA -- TODAY'S TAX SHELTER, TOMORROW'S SECURITY
            (Advantages of IRA accounts.)

(This is a self-mailer, so the bottom panel of the fourth page has space for address and mail indicia.)

This is typical content for a manufacturer's customer newsletter:

Page 1:   WANT TO CUT PRODUCTION COSTS UP TO 40%?
            (How one of the company's products can save money for the customer.)

          TLC IN ACTION
            (How careful quality control and concerned employees have paid off in better performance for customers.)

Page 2:   NEW PORTABLE FILTRATION SYSTEM
            (New product introduction.)

          CLOSED-CENTER HYDRAULIC SYSTEMS
            (Explanation of technical subject by company's Chief Engineer.)

(OUR COMPANY) NAMED "SUPPLIER OF THE YEAR"
> (Award made to company by one of its suppliers. This is basically the same story used in the employee newsletter shown in Chapter VI.)

Page 3: TALKING TO A COMPUTER
> (Explaining how new computer system will affect customers.)

THE FACE YOU ALMOST NEVER SEE
> (Profile of the V.P. Finance.)

OUR OLDEST DISTRIBUTOR
> (Profile of a company sales organization.)

Page 4: ABC COMPANY INSTALLS OVERHEAD CENTRAL TEST SYSTEM
> (How a customer is using company's products.)

SILENCE IS GOLDEN AT CUMBERLAND
> (Another case history story.)

WHAT'S YOUR SOLUTION?
> (Posing a technical problem and including a coupon for customer response.)

Contacts

A customer newsletter generally starts in the Marketing or Sales department, since they're the people most concerned with customers; however, that's not a hard-and-fast rule (there aren't any), since the company president may instigate the idea and want to be presented as the Editor. Unless he's a salesman, though, he's not the best possible Key contact, and he's the most likely to lose interest in the whole thing as he gets busier and involved in other ideas. If you must start with him, try to set up a regular "sub-key" contact in the Marketing department, and let him know you'll depend on him heavily.

You'll also want contacts in Engineering and Personnel for regular contributions, and will probably need other special people each issue for clarification and further information on your stories. Set these up with your key (or sub-key) contact. If you're doing profiles, interview the person yourself. You'll pick up much more interesting information than if you rely on the Personnel department's list of facts or a copy of his resume.

NOTES

CHAPTER VIII

ORGANIZATION

Since this is a how-to-write book, not a how-to-produce one, I won't go into getting copy ready for the printer's camera. Your printer can tell you what needs to be done and how to do it, if you are taking on the whole job yourself. In most cases when I accept responsibility for production of a newsletter, I job out the production so that I can spend my own time on researching and writing. Generally I work with an agency or a company which has its own sources for getting the newsletter produced, so I'm only concerned with the issue up to approved copy.

But even as "just" a writer you'll need to know how the finished product will look and how much space you have to fill. These preparations for your own benefit will also make things easier for the production people....which they'll appreciate....and will give your finished product a more professional appearance, as well.

For an "organizer" I generally make a layout or drawing of the publication, sketching an actual-size "dummy" issue with columns of copy, photos, drawings, illustrations, coupons and headlines indicated. This gives me a good idea of how much copy I need, and on which pages the stories will appear: the most important ones on the first page, etc.

In preparing your layout, you'll want to "size" your photos and illustrations. When you write on anything original....which the printer will use to make his camera shot....use <u>blue</u> pencil, since the camera's eye does not pick up blue. This means you can also use blue-lined cross-hatch paper for graphs, etc. If you make marks with any other color, they'll show in the finished product.

A reduced reproduction of an actual organizer is shown at the end of this chapter. It's a copy of the original, which went to the client and will give you a fairly good idea of what information the printer or paste-up man will need, along with what the client needs to see.

Rather than use a newspaper's habit of starting each story wherever the last one ends and continuing on to the next column, I try to keep all of a story together in a block, spreading the headline over two or three partial columns, if necessary. It's easier to read than "turn to page 3, column 3" and I think it looks neater and better organized. However, the content and your own taste will dictate how to lay the stories out. Each story, of course, will be short, to-the-point, and deal with only one subject.

In preparing your layout or organizer, measure the height of the type that will be used for headlines and allow that much vertical space before measuring the space left for copy. To determine how many lines of copy can be fitted into the remaining space, you'll need a sample of the type in which the copy will be set, and you'll have to know how wide and how long your printed columns will be. Most newsletters are set in 10-point type, which is easy to read, so you can figure about 6 lines to an inch of vertical space. The number of characters in a column line will depend on the width of the column, but once this is determined (see below), I then try to type my rough copy as closely as possible to the length of the column line. It gives me an excellent indication of how well my copy will fit, and it's a great help to the typesetter.

If you've never made a character count, here's how it's done:

(1)   Get a sample of the type in which the newsletter will be set -- a solid block, if possible, of any length.

(2)   Count all the characters, spaces and punctuation marks in one line, and make a note at the end of the line of the total. Do this ten times, on ten consecutive lines.

(3)   Add up the total of the ten lines of characters and divide by 10. This tells you the average number of characters in each line of the sample.

(4)   Measure the length of the sample line and divide the number of inches into the average character count for a line. That tells you how many characters there are in an inch of type.

(5)   Decide how wide your newsletter column will be and multiply that number of inches by the number of characters in an inch, determined in (4) above. That tells you how wide to set your typewriter margins.

Here's an example:

(1), (2) The lines of copy in the sample type have the following numbers of characters, spaces and punctuation marks: 61, 60, 63, 62, 60, 60, 61, 62, 59, 58. (Ten lines).

(3) The total number of characters in the ten lines is 606. Divided by 10 = 60.6. Since the problem is usually too many characters rather than too few, I'll use 60 for an average character count per line.

(4) The lines in the sample are 4-1/2" long. 60 divided by 4.25 = 14.1. That means there are 14 characters to an inch in this type style.

(5) The width of a column in my newsletter will be 2-1/2". 14 characters x 2.5" = 35 characters to a column line. Therefore, I'll set my typewriter margins for 35 characters.

Your columns of copy probably won't fit exactly, but you can always trim out words here and there if it's too long (and probably improve your copy, as well!) or "pad" it with a few extra words. It's better to be a little short ("a little short" = a couple of lines), since the production people can space the paragraphs a little farther apart vertically to use up the space. If they end up with way too much copy to fit, they're likely to trim it themselves (to the detriment of your story), or run a piece of it somewhere else in the newsletter where there's extra space (to the detriment of your organizing). Forestall this by getting it as close as possible to the way you want it to appear.

PREPRINT

Member FDIC ⌂ Equal Housing Lending   Volume 1, Number 4 — Fall, 1979

1979 WAS ANOTHER GOOD YEAR,
SAYS MT. BAKER MUTUAL PRESIDENT PAUL HANSON

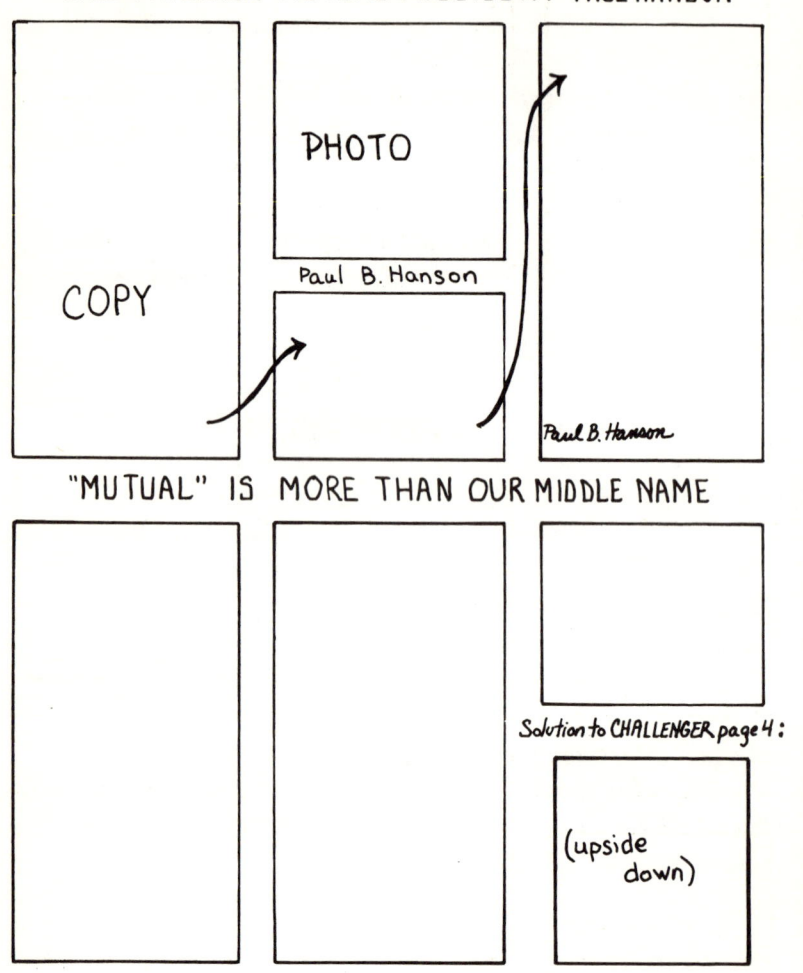

COPY

PHOTO

Paul B. Hanson

Paul B. Hanson

"MUTUAL" IS MORE THAN OUR MIDDLE NAME

Solution to CHALLENGER page 4:

(upside down)

SAV/PLUS WORKS BOTH WAYS FOR MONEY MANAGERS

WE NEVER HEARD A "DUMB QUESTION" ABOUT HOME LOANS

IT'S REALLY SUPER

PASSBOOK ACCOUNTS FOR PRACTICAL PEOPLE

THE COLOR IN YOUR LIFE

$5000

PEOPLE MAKE THE DIFFERENCE

HELP FOR DISMAYED DIETERS

GETTING READY FOR METRICATION.....

IT'S SPRING AGAIN

ACROSS

DOWN

Please put me on the Mutual Mailing list

PREPRINT

NOTES

CHAPTER IX

PRESENTATION

Retype the copy neatly, double-spaced, in the same line length as the rough on which you first typed and "copy-fitted" it (the length of your column line). Put headlines at the top of each story in capital letters, and try to start each story on a new page. This will be helpful to your key contact if some stories have to be approved by several people while others just need one initial.

At the left of the beginning of each story, put a notation as to where the story will appear, i.e., if it's planned to be on Page 1 in the first and second columns, type: "P-1, C-1, 2" in the lefthand margin. Start with the first story on the first page, follow with the <u>second</u> story on page one, and so on.

<u>Be sure to make a carbon</u> of the copy for your own file, or get a Xerox copy made. It will help if you want to make copy changes over the phone, and it will assure that all your work is protected, should the original get lost in the mail or in the approval-cycle.

Submit your layout or organizer with the final copy, and make it as neat as you can. You don't have to be an artist, but give the "approver" something to look at. He may not be a good visualizer. It generally helps to keep a copy of the layout in your file, too -- just in case.

Remember, your copy and layout are your "salesmen" so they should look as businesslike as you <u>are</u>.

Example of final typed copy:

Copy for: Puget Mutual Savings Bank
         Newsletter: Volume XI, Number 6

SUPER SAVER

<u>Super Flexibility and Super Earnings</u>

Puget Mutual's new Super Saver account gives you all the higher earnings advantages of a Certificate of Deposit (CD) plus much of the flexibility of a regular passbook account. 5.75% annual interest rate and 6.0% annual yield without tying up your money for long periods of time. It's a SUPER investment for savers who want to earn more with their money, but like to have it readily available.

<u>Super Flexibility</u>

While your SUPER SAVER account is actually a time deposit, it has some unusual advantages. You can deposit funds to your SUPER SAVER account whenever you like..... there's no minimum deposit required (although we request that you deposit at least $10 when you open the account) and no minimum balance.

In order to earn this higher interest rate, funds deposited to a SUPER SAVER account must remain on deposit for one full calendar quarter (January 1 to March 31, April 1 to June 30, July 1 to September 30, or October 1 to December 31), after which they're available for withdrawal during the first ten days of the following quarter and of each quarter thereafter.

Super Earnings

If you choose to leave your earned interest in your SUPER SAVER account, our policy of compounding interest every day means we'll actually be paying you interest on interest. And because your SUPER SAVER funds earn their entire 5.75% interest in 360 days, you'll get five days <u>extra</u> interest when they're on deposit for a full 365-day year.

Super Investment

In addition to the higher earnings and greater flexibility of the SUPER SAVER account, it's also excellent collateral for a loan. Of course, there are no fees involved with investing in your SUPER SAVER, and each of our depositors is insured up to $40,000 by the FDIC.

For Puget Mutual savers, SUPER SAVER can be the very best of two worlds!

# # #

Samples

Whether you're writing your own company's newsletter or are a freelance writer working for several companies, you should keep a complete file of all issues of every newsletter. If you're a freelancer, it helps to persuade new clients to take a flyer if they can see what other people are doing, and it establishes your competence when you can show tangible proof of your accomplishments.

If you're an "inside" writer, you'll want a complete chronological file of your newsletter on hand in case you want to go back to an earlier subject and expand on it, refer in a current issue to an earlier issue, avoid duplication of information, or make extra copies for late-comers.

Also, if you're publishing more than one type of newsletter for a single company, or writing the same type of newsletter for several companies, the old issues will often provide inspiration for new subject matter.

NOTES

CHAPTER X

A NOTE TO FREELANCE WRITERS

Company newsletters aren't difficult to sell, since their main drawback in a company's thinking is the time and effort they take....time away from the job, if they use a company employee to write the publication(s). When you show that you can save them all this hassle and provide a service of real value....improve employee morale, help their sales force sell, or keep their name before their customers....they're usually willing to listen.

Try to make your proposal to the Sales or Marketing Manager. Ask for an initial interview to see how they sell, what their products and problems are, how many employees they have, who their customers are, and what facilities they have for production (advertising agency, inhouse art department, regular printer, etc.). Then look over your notes and do some hard thinking. What kind of newsletter do they need <u>most</u>, and how much can they afford to pay? Should it <u>be</u> a combined newsletter for two groups, or two separate ones? Put yourself in their shoes, and try to recommend what you'd be willing to buy.

Now try to estimate costs....at least ballpark costs....on production. Most printers can give you a reasonably close estimate if you tell them the size of the publication you're considering, the number of pages, type of paper, number of half-tones, etc. Estimate your time involved in researching, writing, getting approvals and overseeing production, and determine an hourly rate to apply to this time. Then come up with a flat rate per issue for your time. Remember that each issue will take less time as you become more familiar with the client and his business. It's not fair to charge him for your learning time....that will be amortized over a number of issues.

I generally present my estimate in two parts: my own time and production time, depending on how it's to be produced. When you return to the prospective client with your proposal, have a list of possible subjects ready and a cost breakdown on your recommendation. Give him several options, i.e., one newsletter, two separate ones, costs of a two-page typewritten job as opposed to a typeset, four-page newspaper.

Often the best way is to get the thing started as inexpensively as possible, and then, when it's established, upgrade it. I've also found that once a sales newsletter gets underway, the company gets interested in an employee newsletter as well, or a customer publication -- or both.

Another good source of business is advertising agencies. They're usually not geared for this type of work, although many of their clients would like to have newsletters, so they may be willing to have you do all their newsletter work. (I work both ways.....directly with clients and with their agencies, and have excellent relationships with all of them. The agencies, in fact, have been great sources for new work.)

It's almost impossible to suggest actual prices, they can vary so widely with your area, competitive costs, inflation, etc. In the large metropolitan areas you can charge a higher hourly rate than in smaller towns, where clients are generally not as accustomed to the advertising business and its costs.

To be fair, I generally have two hourly rates: a lower one for such activities as proofreading, getting approvals, etc., and a higher one for creative work such as research, copywriting, illustrations, photographic time, etc. At the moment (1979) I estimate my time at $35 per hour for creative work and $10 per hour for administrative time. Depending on the amount of work involved, a publication might cost a client anywhere from $400 per issue to $750, plus production costs. If you're just starting out, you may want to charge less, or if you're an experienced writer in an area that's more sophisticated, by all means charge more. It's easier to get a higher rate when you begin than to try to raise your prices later when you're still doing the same things for the client. Oddly enough, he's willing to admit that inflation affects the cost of materials -- but not the cost of time!

Fortunately, I have sophisticated clients and excellent rapport with them. They generally suggest an occasional raise before I have to ask for it.

Company newsletters are a natural tie-in with a news release program (you have read my book on How To Write News Releases That SELL, haven't you?) since much of the material you gather for a newsletter will make good news releases, and vice-versa. The more complete your package, the more attractive it will be to a potential client -- company or agency.

NOTES

NOTES